A WINNING SKILLS BOOK

You Can Attain Your Goals!

Joy Berry

Illustrated by Bartholomew

Enterprises

Copyright © Joy Berry, 2022
Originally Published 2013

All rights are reserved.

No part of this book can be duplicated or used without the prior written permission of the copyright owner, except for the use of brief quotations from the book.

For inquiries or permission requests contact the publisher.

Published by Joy Berry Enterprises
www.joyberryenterprises.com

You can get what you want if you understand
- desires and goals,
- four steps to achieving goals,
- eight obstacles to achieving goals,
- ten qualities of achievers, and
- how to become an achiever.

INTRODUCTION

If you are like most people, you have **desires**. Your desires are the things you would like to be, do, or have.

If you desire things enough to do whatever is necessary to get them, your desires become **goals.**

A goal is something a person wants and tries to achieve.

DESIRES AND GOALS

There are two basic kinds of goals.

Short-term goals usually require a minimum amount of effort and can be achieved in a short time.

Long-term goals usually require more effort and can be achieved only over a longer period of time.

DESIRES AND GOALS

Sometimes it is necessary to achieve several short-term goals in order to achieve a long-term goal.

Usually, the effort and time invested in achieving a goal are proportionate to the benefits derived from achieving the goal. The greater the investment of effort and time, the greater the reward.

DESIRES AND GOALS

You can achieve any goal as long as you are **able and willing** to make it happen.

To achieve a goal you must be physically and mentally capable of achieving it.

DESIRES AND GOALS

To achieve a goal you must be willing to do whatever is necessary to make it happen.

FOUR STEPS TO ACHIEVING GOALS

Achieving a goal is easier when you follow four basic steps.

Step 1: Define the goal.

Establish exactly what is your goal. Avoid general goals such as "I want to be happy" or "I want to be successful." Instead, try to be specific.

Specific goals represent particular accomplishments. For example, learning how to do a particular task or acquiring something in particular is a specific goal.

Having specific goals makes it easier to determine exactly what needs to be done to achieve them.

Step 2: Make a list.

List the tasks that need to be done to achieve the goal.

It might be beneficial to have someone help you make the list.

Talk to a person who is experienced in setting and achieving goals.

Or, talk to a person who has achieved a goal that is similar to yours.

Step 3: Organize the list.

List the tasks in order of how they need to be accomplished. List what needs to be done first, second, third, and so on.

It might be helpful to list each task on a small slip of paper. Place the slips on a flat surface. Organize them in a vertical row with the first task at the top of the row and the last task at the bottom.

Copy the list of tasks in proper order onto a sheet of paper. This will become a "Things to Do" list.

FOUR STEPS TO ACHIEVING GOALS

Step 4: Do each task.

Work from the "Things to Do" list and do whatever needs to be done to achieve the goal.

Start from the top of the list and complete each task in order.

When you complete a task, cross it off your list and move on to the next task.

Keep going until you have crossed off every task on the list. At this point you will have achieved your goal.

Sometimes you might not want to do a task on the "Things to Do" list. However, to achieve your goal, sometimes it is necessary to do things you might not want to do.

Avoid procrastinating.

Do not put off doing a job. Do it as soon as possible.

Avoid escaping.

Do not try to get out of doing a task by doing something else. Focus your attention on the task that needs to be done and stick with the job until it is finished.

Here are some things you can do to make an undesirable task easier to accomplish.

Race with the clock.

Set a time limit for the task. Then try to get the job done in the allotted time or sooner.

Reward yourself.

Promise yourself you will do something you truly enjoy after you finish the task. Then keep the promise you made to yourself.

EIGHT OBSTACLES TO ACHIEVING GOALS

Here are several obstacles that can make achieving your goals difficult. It is important for you to overcome these obstacles if you are going to get what you want.

Obstacle 1. Negative people

Some people might not believe you are capable of achieving your goals. Others might think your goals are impossible to achieve. People who have these negative thoughts can influence you to think as they do. This can damage your self-confidence and make it difficult for you to achieve your goals.

It is important for you to avoid being around people who have negative thoughts about you and your goals.

Obstacle 2. Nonsupportive people

Some people who have less than you might be critical or jealous of you. This can make you feel bad.

Some people who have more than you might be judgmental and feel superior to you. This can make you feel bad.

Bad feelings can keep you from achieving your goals.

You need to develop worthwhile values. Then you need to develop relationships with people who support those values.

Obstacle 3. Worry

It takes time to worry. It also takes physical, mental, and emotional energy. In spite of this, worrying seldom accomplishes anything positive. It only upsets you and keeps you from achieving your goals.

The time and energy you use worrying are not used to do what you need to do. Therefore, you should not waste your time or energy worrying. Instead, focus on achieving your goals.

Obstacle 4. Indecision

Deciding what to do is the first step toward achieving a goal. If you do not take this first step, you cannot take the other necessary steps and the result will be doing nothing at all.

You might be indecisive because you are afraid you will make the wrong decision and fail. However, in most cases the most effective way to know whether a decision is right or wrong is to act on it.

You might need to try many things before you reach the right decision.

Obstacle 5. Laziness

Achieving a goal takes work. Many people do not want to work. They are lazy.

Laziness can turn you into a passive person who waits for things to happen instead of an active person who causes things to happen. Laziness might make you pass up an opportunity to get what you want if that opportunity requires some effort.

If you want to achieve your goals, you must take advantage of every opportunity that comes you way. You must be willing to work.

Obstacle 6. Overdependence on others

Many people do not want to work to achieve their goals. They would rather depend on someone else to do or get things for them.

Depending on others can be frustrating because you have no control over them. You cannot be sure they will come through for you.

The only person over whom you have complete control is yourself. If you learn to work to get the things you want, you will not be completely dependent on others and you will gain more control over your own situation.

Obstacle 7. Mistreating others

It will be impossible for you to accomplish all of your goals all by yourself. Sometimes you will need other people to help you. People will be more willing to help you if you are honest and fair.

To be sure that you are honest and fair, you need to treat other people the way you want to be treated.

Obstacle 8. Dissatisfaction

Achieving goals will not make you happy unless you learn to appreciate what you have. You will not be happy if all of your thoughts are focused on the things you do not have. You will not be happy if you are always feeling that you do not have enough.

You must focus on what you *do* have, rather than what you *do not have*. This will help you enjoy your achievements and will make you feel that your efforts are worthwhile.

TEN QUALITIES OF ACHIEVERS

If you achieve your goals, you will become an achiever. Achievers are people who reach their goals. Achievers share many positive qualities.

Quality #1—Motivation

Achievers have a strong desire to achieve their goals.

Quality #2—Confidence

Achievers believe in themselves. They realize they have the potential to achieve many things. They believe they can do almost anything they decide to do.

Quality #3—Open-mindedness

Achievers are willing to listen to others and learn from them. Before they do anything, they consider the advice they get from trustworthy people.

Quality #4—Flexibility

Achievers are willing to change when they find a way to improve. They are also willing to change their plans when they discover a better way to accomplish their goals.

Quality #5—Courage

Achievers are willing to take a chance. They make an effort to achieve their goals, even though they might fail or be criticized by others.

Quality #6—Initiative

Achievers are ambitious. They never put off what needs to be done. They do every task as soon as possible.

Achievers work independently. They try not to depend on others to get them started or keep them going.

Quality #7—Conscientiousness

Achievers are conscientious. They give their very best effort to whatever they attempt to do. No matter how large or how small the task, they do the best job they can do.

Quality #8—Discipline

Achievers are willing to give up something they enjoy if it could keep them from achieving their goals.

They are also willing to do things they might not want to do if it will help them achieve their goals.

Quality #9—Concentration

Achievers do not allow things to distract them or keep them from doing what they need to do.

They focus their attention and efforts on achieving their goals.

Quality #10—Perseverance

Achievers keep going. If what they are doing is right, they never give up.

You can achieve your goals if you
- are able and willing,
- follow the four steps to achieving goals,
- overcome the eight obstacles that might keep you from achieving your goals, and
- nurture the ten qualities that will make you an achiever.

People who achieve very few things are called underachievers.

People who do not achieve goals are nonachievers.

BECOMING AN ACHIEVER

People are not *born* achievers, underachievers, or nonachievers.

People *become* achievers, underachievers, or nonachievers.

CONCLUSION

You can become an achiever if you choose to be one and do whatever is necessary to achieve your goals. This means that getting what you want is up to you!

www.ingramcontent.com/pod-product-compliance
Lightning Source LLC
Chambersburg PA
CBHW081408070526
44583CB00020B/2721